Symphony in Monotony

Tarun Saini

BookLeaf
Publishing

India | USA | UK

Presentation by *BookLeaf Publishing*

Web: www.bookleafpub.com

E-mail: info@bookleafpub.com

ISBN: 9789358739381

First edition 2024

Dedicated to my family, teachers and two phenomenal guides namely Life and Time

INDEX

PART I
The Storm Within

Monotony: The Realization

Does the changing calendar and clicking clock
scare you?
Am I meant for this or should have scaled
higher?
Or am I condemned to the abyss with nothing in
sight new?
Have little I got yet don't know what to desire

A sense deep within of being empty,
Yet a feeling of doused fire inside for I'm
already full;
Not at peace with my present, can't see future
with certainty
Some solace, some griefs of past which without
efforts pull

Some called it fatigue, others termed it anxiety,
The more I discussed, got for the ailment names
newer;
Finally reached my wise elusive guide who
pronounced, "Monotony",
"It's the daily life that excites you no longer"

"I want to fix it now", I both demanded and implored,
"I think I should change my job", I wondered;
"For that's where I spend most of my awake hours", I explored
"A newer work field will change my view", I summarized

He smiled, "So, it's the work which is a burden, rest all is a cruise",
"Be honest, till the time you are in doubt, it would persist";
I was rattled, "No, actually I don't like anything, work was a ruse"
He again smiled, "Think about everything, don't resist"

This time I was more settled, "May be to myself I need to pamper",
"Been times that have been to a good holiday or bought a new device"
This time was smile wider, "And you have done that in the past never?"
"Should you fix symptoms without touching the cause," was his question precise

"I should try to spend more time with family," I
did grudgingly speak,
"Sure, you should, but can a sad man bring
happiness to family?"
And this statement made my slumber break
Even with family I have been and not been there
really

He stood up, "Take your time but there's
someone you should meet",
"It's half past 6, we may catch her, it's still not
dark"
Seeing him rush out, I too followed him on feet
In no time we were in a neighborhood park

The park was crowded but it appeared we were
looking for someone special,
Took him a few seconds before he yelled her
name;
"Antara," he was looking towards the bicycle
path peripheral,
A rider raised her hand and smiling she came

"Who is she", wondered me curious,
"See for yourself, in a while", told the master
wise;
"Aha! Always good to see you," chuckled the
girl gregarious,
"Sorry, my name is Antara!", the girl waived at
me in no time

"So, I have a favor to ask you, he's my friend,"
told my guide
"He is old to the city but wants to try something
new;
Can he join your group in the morning for the
ride?"
Antara giggled, "Done! But tell me he isn't as
boring as you?"

Wait! Are they talking about me and deciding?
I haven't spoken a word and haven't given my
mind;
And like a school kid been put in course
certainly not my liking,
Didn't want to say anything then so just smiled

"So see you tomorrow an hour after the
sunlight"
Still didn't say anything but feebly waived;
And did burst when she went out of sight,
"I have not come for a cycle ride", I said in
voice raised

Calmly responded the wise man, "I know",
"But pray tell me, your impression of her
through this meeting brief";
I quipped, "Rich woman in early 30s, happy,
joyful as it did show",
Laughed the wise guide,"Well, she's older, got a
so called boring job and even some grief"

He continued, "The step first to salvation is
realisation",
"For it is purposeless to walk if you don't know
the way";
"Sometimes in others we can see both our
problems and their solution",
I nodded, "I will meet her group tomorrow at the
start of the day."

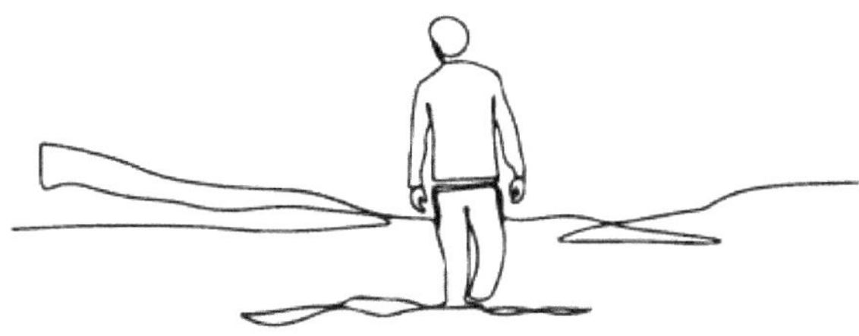

Monotony: The Ride Away & Within

In a day I was to start with this group I didn't
know,
Arranged a bike from someone who once was an
enthusiast;
I was anxious, hesitant and a feeling of unease
began to grow,
So while I would go, I didn't know if this
experiment would last

While setting the alarm, I realised there was no
precise time mentioned,
It was a vague description if I correctly recalled
exact;
"An hour after the light," in my mind echoed,
So after ages looked for time of sunrise the day
next

I was greeted by seven cyclists as I reached the
point,
Mixed age group, varied appearances but had the
same energy;
And like school kids they raced as if got a flag to
hoist,
I soon trailed but then Antara came and offered a
remedy

"We'll use shortcut", she told me smiling slyly,
"Wouldn't they know", I tried to control my grin
broad;
"Well, they are too busy competing blindly",
And our bikes moved to a path alternate off the
road

"It is not a smooth one and looks like it will
never end", I was exhausting,
She laughed, "When is all smooth buddy, don't
focus on road but the ride";
I protested, "It's hard to focus when the path is
rough and never ending",
"Navigate the rough, and please remember
nothing ever lasts", she said with smile wide

In a few moments we were at a stop
intermediate,
Antara calmly asked, "Did you see those big
bamboo shoots in our way?"
"What shoots, I didn't see any", was my reaction
immediate,
She chuckled, "So you missed things taller than
us in the broad day?"

I was getting agitated, "All of it looked the
same",
"Or is it that we choose to see so", she said
calmly exhaling,
She continued, "You could see flowers, creepers,
trees of countless types as we came"
"May be the beauty hides in front of us and we
term it common and boring"

We caught up with the group soon and
eventually the ride got over,
I was thrilled and was already eager for the day
next;
"When do we meet tomorrow", I asked sounding
bolder,
She laughed, "Same time but the minutes change
in exact"

I was amused, "Why such a schedule of hour
after sunlight",
"Why not tell a time specific"
She smiled, "Because through this even an
ordinary meeting time brings delight"
"Tell me, last when did you plan to reach
somewhere 27 minutes past Six"

I saw today what I always chose to ignore,
Does there lie a hidden meaning in what as
ordinary we counted?
Do we really see things as they are pure?
And may be everything boring doesn't need to
be discounted

I slept well that night with a reason to wake up
excited,
The thing wasn't new but a perspective was
sinking in;
I still have doubts but a few things I've decided,
Look forward to a ride away and ride within.

Monotony & Perfection

Been over a month now and I'm sitting again
with the guide,
But I'm calmer, happier and less anxious;
Sensed he also, "Seems you're liking the ride"
I smiled but I still had few doubts vicious

"What if I again get bored with this approach",
"What if gets lost the desire to see differently", I
was apprehensive;
Cautiously spoke as I was wary of his reproach
He looked in my eyes, "Look at the picture
comprehensive"

"Let us buy something", suddenly he got up,
And like earlier, I also rushed;
But now I was excited and not fearing snub,
For looks that my doubt can get flushed

We found ourselves at gates of a lavish store,
It's known to be the biggest name for fabric
exotic;
People flock for valuable sarees, shawls and
more
Exquisite pieces with guarantees of being
authentic

In a moment, our wise man was holding a cloth
exceptional,
It was the prized Pashmina shawl from land of
Kashmir;
The cloth carried legacy of artwork since times
immemorial,
The appearance was splendid, the quality none
else could come near

"Can see in your eyes that you too find it good",
he whispered,
I agreed, "Not amazed at the price it
commands";
"But not sure if you know the work behind,"
said the wizard,
"Toil, patience, skill, discipline and monotony it
demands"

I was in disbelief, "You are not saying to just
quell my storm?"
He beamed, "Well, you should know this
process certainly";
"For it is layered in human victory through
imagination and resolve firm"
"Right from thread to this art piece, there lies a
story"

With infinite patience is collected the thinnest
wool,
The yarn gets wrapped with high skill and
immense labor;
The color is done with care bountiful
And unparalleled is the precision of the art
maker

The course runs for months and not weeks and
days,
The knowledge is passed through generations;
Perfection blesses dedication and there are no
alternate ways
Some routes to success need imagination and
repetitions

Do ask yourself a question sincere,
Have you lost all means to race to the perfection;
Or you want to hide behind change as excuse
mere
Because what you call monotony may just be a
road to perfection

Monotony & Victory

I received a message at night from the wise
master,
To reach his home before the sunrise;
Any questions to be discussed only thereafter,
And I reached the place at time precise

"We should go for a drive", he commanded,
"Let's go through the old city road and then to
the stadium"
"Why to these places, at this hour", I resisted
But he insisted, "To see these places as a
different medium"

We reached the old city and saw a world
different,
There were traders, shopkeepers and
transporters;
Milk, fruits, vegetables and a lot of other goods
significant,
Being loaded and transported across city's
corners

"When we sleep, what actually runs life moves
in the city"
"And this is done every day, without failing
since memory serves"
"Not everything is done for interest and joy but
also as responsibility"
"Imagine, if every monotonous work is treated
unworthy", were his words

We reached the stadium cruising through streets
empty,
But inside was like a shopping mall;
Hoards and scores of athletes running and
exercising in every vicinity,
And they were all ages, be pro or just beginners
small

I heard him going somber first time,
"See this place, it will be excellence's cradle;
It will produce talent and quality prime
Those who repeatedly toil today , for country
will bring medal"

He continued, "See, these who we see today
perspiring,
Repeating the routine and stretching it far
Would one day be figures inspiring
For they have conquered fears, doubts and
monotony beyond par"

I saw a teen sweating in otherwise weather cold,
Saw a small one keenly following her coach's
direction;
Saw another one falling badly, yet got up bold,
No boredom, no fear, just plain conviction

As we returned, I was the one speaking,
"I have understood what you wanted me to see;
Even monotony has excellence, purpose and
meaning,
And it can be seen in life", the wise guide
smiled, "I agree!"

PART Ⅱ
The Drizzle of Life

The 3 Minute Traffic Light

Long ride back home and I have gotten late,
Heart wants to fly, mind to race but traffic could
only crawl;
A long day just again got longer; Can only curse
the fate,
Further the heart sank as I heard the rain fall.

The sea of cars moved in one direction and so
did mine,
Hands on the wheel, jaw stiff and target on sight;
Prayers on lips, want to cross the line,
Can't get stuck at the 3-minute traffic light

But screeched the car ahead and just before,
Time and luck didn't favor; I've seen it again,
Rolled windows down and glanced to right as
heard a V8 roar,
Oh Man! Life this is, rest all is a meaningless
pain.

Couldn't take my eyes off but saw the rider's
smirk,
Quickly looked to the other side and there was a
world inverse;
A woman, a child in a cycle rickshaw pulled by
a man with no perks,
And laughing were all three, talking happily in
their universe.

"Thank God, you came! Was thinking of
walking in rain,"
"No! That wouldn't have been wise," countered
the man who pedalled;
"Mummy, papa brought me to hold the
umbrella," the kid exclaimed,
God! This is a family, in a no fancy world.

"You didn't tell me he came 4th in the class," the
man resented,
"You promised a toy for 1st," said she in tone
light;
"Ha! 4 is bigger than 1," laughed everyone as
said the man contended,
As turned the light green, I saw this rich family
on the road go out of sight.

A while back everything mine I was resenting,
Then was jealous of the machine of a man I
didn't know;
And this family is happy getting drenched in
drizzling,
Smiling even when the means are lowest of the
low.

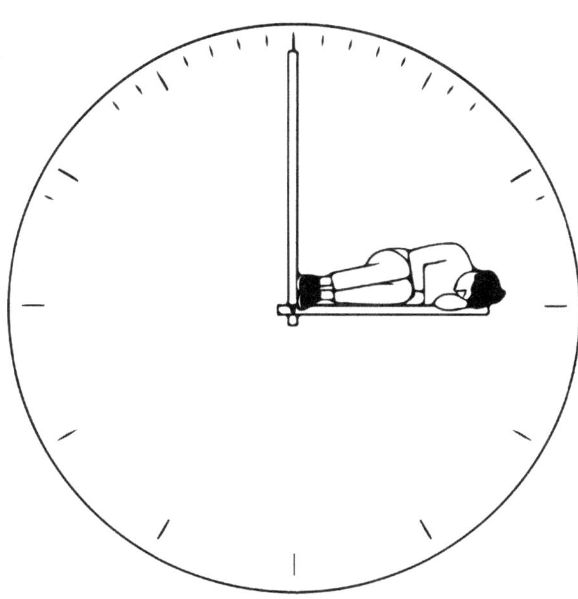

That Unplanned Travel

"The flight's cancelled? So make arrangements
alternate,"
My anger on the travel desk was distinct and
visible;
"Sir, there was only one direct flight on the
route," said the executive in tone moderate,
"But you can take a flight halfway and then an
overnight train is possible

"Overnight Train?" And a picture flashed before
me, yes like you are seeing!
"Please try something else," now my tone
became softer;
"Sir, based on your travel dates, this is the only
option for the time being,"
I resigned to fate, understanding it's no use to
argue any longer.

We humans live in past and future,
We remember the yesterday and imagine the
tomorrow;
So a bad train travel years ago is still in mind,
that's the nature,
And that I have to travel again, filled even my
flight before with sorrow.

Physically reached the railway station at night
half past eight,
Though mentally I had reached here 3 days
before;
Quickly looked for the waiting room and picked
a seat as for train I waited,
Had this travel not been paramount, wouldn't
have cared to explore.

On the display showed arrival in 10 minutes on
platform number two,
Hurriedly rushed as can't even imagine to miss
the boarding;
Cleaner platforms, organized stalls were there
but were not for my view,
I crossed the overbridge in seconds and reached
my spot gasping.

"There's still time sir, easy!" I heard a voice
from behind,
He was a vendor at a stall, "It stops for 5
minutes,"
Did I ask him for advice, why can't his own
business he mind?
As I caught my breath, I looked at him selling
tea, water, chips, biscuits.

"Take some water!" said the man appearing
candid,
He was right, so I picked up a bottle, "Where
does AC First Class arrive?"
"Just 10 steps," as he spoke my eyes got fixed
on a photo frame garlanded,
"Isn't he Shamsher Singh ji?" I asked, he
nodded yes with surprise.

"So you are his son Jagjit, we studied together,"
my voice trembled with joy,
"What a fool I am," my ex-class fellow stepped
out and hugged me tight;
A lifetime ago and hundreds of miles away, our
families lived close by,
Just then, Jagjit moved away suddenly, realizing
holding me was not right.

"You have become AC First class," he tried to
joke as if hiding a mistake,
"All that matters is that class of '98'," I
continued to hold him;
"But how has all this happened?" I feebly asked
for it was difficult to take,
He laughs, "Some tides of time! But things
aren't so grim."

He pushed me aside, "Let me make tea for you,"
And quickly started moving his hands, "Thanks
to uncle's photo," I said.
"You look so different; I couldn't have
recognized you,"
"As if you are still that 100m sprinter of school,"
he said and I agreed.

"This tea is better than what you would get in
your office place,"
I sipped and it did taste like never before;
In bliss, continued taking sips, just when the
whistle brought me to the base,
"Tell me your number, I'm sending you mine," I
said with delay no more.

The train stopped exactly at the same spot as he
mentioned,
Jagjit snatched my bag and carried with me till
my seat;
Placed it rightly and then did something out of
comprehension,
Stepped down the train and vanished without a
greeting.

Just when the train was about to start, he again
appeared with a bag brown,
"There's no food service in train, so eat these if
in need,"
The train whistled again, we could feebly
embrace and then Jagjit got down,
I waved him through the window and then the
train gained speed.

Decided to check the bag, it had chips, biscuits,
water and a tiffin,
The old steel box with his name written, must
have been his dinner;
The one to me he had given,
Suddenly, to me things appeared hazy, my eyes
had two drops of water.

I pulled my phone and started typing mail to the
travel agent,
I want same route to return and not direct flight;
Called my wife that return journey has got
longer, came up something urgent,
I opened the tiffin, while my wet glasses
continued to trouble with sight.

The Question Paper

"How was the exam, honey?" I asked the first
thing after seeing my girl of nine,
"Very good! Just that there was a confusing
question in the middle,"
"Bring the question paper, let me see," I
demanded hiding curiosity of mine,
I helped her prepare thoroughly, did I miss a
needle?

"Here it is! Question number six,"
I turned the leaf and my eyes quickly skipped
through the rest;
And then they widened, it was a package of
tricks,
"How did you attempt this?" I asked, hiding my
emotions best.

"Papa, I read it and read it again, but couldn't
find the solution,"
"So I left it for then and finished the rest of the
questions,
Then came back, I just got the idea that it is a
question of combination."
"Excellent!" said I, overjoyed, "Who gave you
these suggestions?"

"The teacher asked us to spend time on page
one, before we write,"
I turned the leaf back, it was the page of
instructions;
A page which is the first but generally out of
sight,
"Papa! it says on point 3 not to waste too much
time over any question."

And it crossed my mind if it isn't the case with
everything we stare at,
I sat down on the chair, this page merited a
deeper reading;
On top was mentioned, to read the questions
with care,
Answers exist, questions aren't wrong, have
been put after thorough checking.

Point No. 2 was about clean and clear
expression,
Separate the rough from the fair and answer
clearly;
Final answer to be brief and without confusion,
Clutter won't count and in fact can cost dearly.

Point No. 3 said all questions carry same marks,
So if don't know one, move on to other, don't
waste the session;
Finish off the rest and then you can come back,
You are here for the full exam, not to conquer
just one question.

Isn't life an exam, but instructions do I read?
Have jumped on conclusions, expressed
chaotically before delving fine;
Questioned the issues, questioned the outcomes
but not own deed,
But relevant most is point no. 3 for both a girl of
nine and me at thirty-nine.

Not everything is as valuable as we perceive,
Need to move over one or any obsession;
The newer avenues await if wholeheartedly we
receive,
No one event can decide the fate without
redemption.

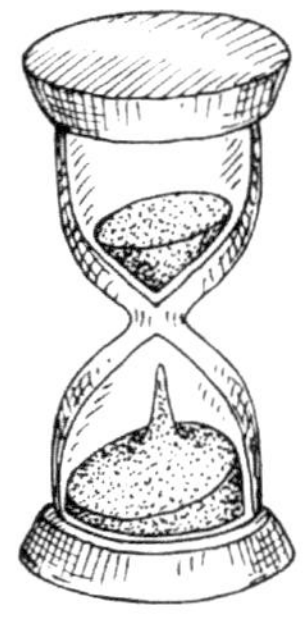

A Visit To The Park

What's your idea of a nice Sunday morning?
A long sleep, late breakfast, an old book can be
part of list,
But mine had a different start and ending,
It started with "Papa let's go to park", that's the
gist.

Pulled out of a nice sleep, found myself amongst
grass, flowers and bushes.
There was a set of those who value health
breezing past,
Some jogging, some walking and some were on
pushes,
The kid vanished in a group of kids around
swings, before even a moment was lost.

I first tried to walk amongst the old, but they
were too slow,
Then looked at the group jogging with brisk
pace,
Lost out to them and had to step out of the flow,
So started walking on grass to save the face.

There I saw a man leaning on the flowers,
Gently caressing the stems, touching the leaves
and firmly pressing the ground,
Gardener was he, I could judge through my
observation powers,
But then I saw what can't be called an act of
mind sound.

He was addressing the plants by name, asking
about their state,
Then wished them good health and asked to
leave,
As he was walking, I called him, "Listen mate",
"Were you talking to the plants", I was not ready
to believe.

"Yes sir! They are like children, just look
different and stationary,
We need to understand this if we want to protect
them;
Want to have their trust and so do likewise as is
necessary,
They grow fast and healthy", he summed.

"See all these flowers grew in the last few
weeks", said the voice proud.
"Wonderful, so these plants grow the fastest?" I
asked excited prime.
"Nah sir! Fastest growing plants are there", he
pointed to the children's crowd.
"Cherish them blooming every day if you can,
they grow in no time!"

There I saw the different flowers giggling with
exuberance,
Ages may be different but innocence was the
common thread;
Laughing their hearts out even when nothing
was so humorous,
Let me see this all for now, for adulting is all but
dread.

The Coffee Shop

Those thundering skies, that heavy pour,
That corner table that I booked long before;
Have already read the sms thrice and read once
more,
"Sorry! Will have to skip, there's work I can't
ignore"

I murmured, "Just another addition to the score",
Happened thrice already and it's just increased
to four;
Since last time it was distance, now, closest
places I did explore,
Three hundred yards it was, may be still it was
far as before

The coffee I ordered while waiting now turning
cold,
And there lied a feedback form with four fold;
While I overlooked it and looked beyond the
road,
I saw approaching me, the waiter with smile
broad

"Sir, Hope the drink is up to your taste?"
I didn't want to, still blurted out in haste;
"This is not a coffee but a poor disgrace,
For, it would rank last in any culinary race"

"Do you actually check what you serve?"
"And then you have a feedback form, what a
nerve!"
Could see my words falling like rocks on a
stranger
He whispered, 'sorry', while picking up the
paper

Realities and realisations visit once you're calm,
The words we speak can be both rocks and a
balm
I realised I was unfair to both the store and the
man
So to the counter I didn't walk, I ran

"See, I didn't mean that!", was my first line
"It was something else, your coffee was fine!"
And there came back a smile though feeble,
"Thanks sir, but please do tell even if we missed
by little"

"No, for sure you were good", I tried to reason,
Wanted to cover for my act and not let it deepen;
I continued, "So you get a chance to enjoy
everyday",
"The best coffee and the food, right on your
way"

"Sir, to be really honest, I can't afford the drink"
"It costs nearly half a day salary", he said with a
wink;
"Actually, it's my dream long cherished"
"To sip coffee, look outside the glass with meal
relished"

"To just sit there and look at the weather
outside"
"People seek company but frankly sitting alone
would be no downside"
"And I can be with both past and future at the
same time"
"With a smile on face and thoughts sublime"

"I'm sorry, I got carried away," he apologised,
"Actually, don't be, you have put it rightly," I
smiled;
"What we don't value can be worth a dream"
"Happiness is around us but not necessarily in
way it could seem"

I could see the water stream running on the
glass,
A scene so common yet of such a distinct class
That lightening in the skies above and a hot cup
in my hand
I have my own company, it's no less than a
magic wand

The Oasis

I would ask you a difficult question of present
times,
What is very difficult but equally imperative to
do?
It's got to do with kids, does it ring any chimes?
It's keeping them away from smart devices,
agree won't you?

So we decided to give our daughter a break from
the digital,
She'd read a paperback book daily, that would
be a start right;
While reading she would make notes pivotal,
And so her first book was of stories from
Arabian Nights.

Kids have a curious way to read,
They have a question after every para and
comment after every two lines;
So you have to be with them if you want them to
proceed,
We too realized as in the beginning itself we got
signs.

It was the story of a merchant returning through
the desert vast,
He started feeling thirsty, his loaded camel was
tired,
In search of water his eyes wandered, scanned
the huge sea of sand fast,
And he spotted signs of oasis, and a new
strength he acquired.

"Papa, what is an oasis?" the girl asked
immediately,
"It's a land fertile in the middle of desert," I
simplified;
"It has plants, grass, water and helps travelers", I
summarized swiftly,
"Papa, are oases very far away in desert?" she
enquired.

"Yes they are not very common, the traveler's
luck is on side,
The traveler reaches the oasis and quenches his
thirst;
Rests a bit and then again continues with his
stride
To reach his destination by evening next."

"Wait, wait let me note down the moral and key
point,"
"The story is only half done", I was slightly
annoyed;
But then I realized to a child it's wrong to
disappoint,
"Please tell what are the learnings implied"

The girl speaks, "When in desert, don't lose
hope, there'd be oasis,"
"Second, if not carrying water, what's the use of
loading camel with things other"
"And third, oasis is not final destination, only
means to travel to bases."
Speechless was I, in the desert of life the lesson
is for me the traveller!

Haven't we felt even small events determinant,
Haven't we craved and hoarded for things
meaningless;
Haven't we mistaken every situation to be
permanent,
Was trying to teach the child instead got lessons
priceless.

The Heavy PPT

I don't have stereotypes, but have an observation
about office people's age,
Not about work or quality but when they leave
the office in the evening;
The ones in 20s leave first and the 50s are the
next to leave the stage,
So when you see a near retirement colleague till
9, it's surprising.

"Is it a long day Sharma ji or you've become
inefficient?" I asked joking,
Was no response from the man whose glasses
were about to leave his nose,
His forehead looked stiffer than the traffic of
Monday morning,
Seeing him wiping his sweaty cheeks, I rose.

As I approached him, he saw me with both hope
and despair,
"HO PPT needs to go today only, straight
instruction from the boss,"
Mr. Sharma retires in 4 months and has been
assigned to a team of a young Turk with flair,
How unwanted he would be made to feel
tomorrow, could sense his loss.

"Have you not prepared it?" I asked, "No, it's
not going,"
"I'm trying to send but failing as can't make the
file lighter,"
I looked at the file properties and the number it
was showing,
It was not only heavy, it was a huge 129
Megabytes.

"Sharma ji, this needs surgery, if sending is
must",
"I have tried all I can, can't figure it out," the
sound was bleak.
And he pushed the laptop towards me with both
embarrassment and trust,
And I took it with a sense of favor, though the
problem wasn't unique.

"So many problems, please see", like a doctor I
diagnosed,
"You have added pictures of large sizes and data
files embedded directly.
Why do you need these flimsy animations and
so many slides in annexures?" I posed.
Seeing his blank face as a yes, I operated and
showed the reduced file proudly.

"Thank you so very much", the voice had relief
and joy,
I returned to my seat and started packing but was
startled,
Sharma ji followed me, to get another help, was
it a ploy?
Before I spoke a word, he loudly giggled.

"Thank you for teaching this old man a thing or
two at this hour,"
"You are welcome, Sharma ji", I tried to eat a
humble pie,
"No, you are not getting it, see what a nice
lesson you did shower.
Wish I got this 20 years back", he said with a
sigh.

"Pictures we all portray, we all carry from days
behind and they make us slow,
Animated are our actions, lacking the truth and
simplicity;
Surrounded we are with so much and so many
whose utility is low,
Truncating it is better if we want to grow", said
Sharma ji in brevity.

I liked the thought on what doesn't let us grow, I
wished him night,
The life lesson I didn't want to forget so picked
up to pen it fast;
I have a habit of using acronyms, that's how I
capture what I write,
Sunk a bit deeper when I saw the acronym that
needs handling, it is the PAST.

Let go of all past pictures and you must,
Be yourself and shrug the animated rust;
Lighter would you be with things simple and
people you trust,
Truncating is the path to liberation, learn it first.

The Flat Tyre

The hour hand of the watch was reaching eleven,
And then you realise it's already late in the day;
The pitch dark outside and so hurried as again,
May have spent entire day but now want to
cover on the way

My breath became heavier when reached the car,
It was tilting a bit on one side
Flat tyre it is, could make from far
Nearly midnight, and here goes off my ride

One can expect no one for assistance at that
hour,
It's been fairly long that I changed on own
Yet decided to try on own as help was certainly
far;
While even not sure if the spare wheel too
wasn't gone

As I pulled the tools, an old man approached,
"Need help?", said that man in guard's uniform;
"Can you?", I said considering his age advanced,
"Well, sir, two are better than one," he did affirm

"A flat tyre at this hour!", I was frustrated,
Was trying extra hard yet was not getting the
desired result
"Sir, may I suggest! It's not complicated",
"First rule is accepting the state; it works as
occult"

He continued, "There's no apt time for crisis
emergence"
"It will come when it has to and come it will";
"It's the prep beforehand that determines
resurgence"
"And whatever it is try to get the thrill"

I smiled as didn't want to obstruct his flow
"Second, you need are some right tools at hand";
"You need some help with lifting but do it
slow",
"But before that just loosen the faulty wheel on
the stand"

I could see neither frustration nor force was
used,
Cool head, firm hands and right tools worked
fine;
In minutes, the faulty wheel made way as I was
bemused
Now the spare needs to be placed in line

"Sir, these small holes need special respect",
"For the wheel will not just go just like that";
"The nuts and bolt need alignment in all aspect"
And once done, the new wheel got fixed in an
instant

The loosening and tightening takes place with
same tool
But what varies is the direction
It is what distinguishes wise from the fool
The secret lies in the choice and the selection

I couldn't thank enough the man for help and
lesson
Was on my way with worthy advice to admire
You can't prevent the crisis but its impact can
lessen
In all aspects of life learn to fix a flat tyre

The 4 PM Tea

"Bhatia, work extra for 10 minutes in evening, but
now come", I fumed,
"Coming man, seems sir's day is not as per plan",
Bhatia joked;
"It's as any Monday could be, but you also need
that cup, I assumed",
This ended any debate and we both quietly walked.

Across the road was our destination, a small tea
shop,
Frequented by office goers for a quick tasty sip;
And some fresh air or to start thinking or to stop,
Much rested everyday on this small 4 PM trip.

"I think economy needs another rate hike", I
quipped
"Yes, and you think our salary would increase
equally", He scorned;
"Nah! We don't fall in that list of automatic
increase", I sipped,
"Typical middle class, typical middle-aged", We
mourned.

"I think, I should have taken the Bangalore offer",
"Didn't I tell you the same?"
"Yes you did, and I told you about how rigid was
HR's proffer",
"Well, you go anywhere but this job family would
still be the same."

"Role, money, place, family needs all run in
different directions", I was dejected,
"Maybe we don't exactly know what we need," he
said with a tight lip;
"Maybe peace is all what I need", I reflected,
"My friend, maybe we are already holding it", he
said as he took the longest sip.

The small victories during the day, the little battles
we fight,
The silver linings of future, the great past's sorrow
All find space in this small cup we hold tight,
As if saying, "Smile, there's still a today, there's
still a tomorrow."

What's for Dinner

Mom, I just had a four-course meal,
In a place where bookings go beyond days and
weeks,
A place where they say you don't eat the food,
you actually feel,
And yet in the palace of my mind a memory
sneaks.

Was it better than our dining table which was
half covered with random stuff?
Did someone wait for me even when I was two
hours late?
Did someone insist on that one extra roti and
pushed rough?
Did someone tell that I didn't eat anything even
after seeing empty plate?

Did someone pick the 3 softest rotis from the
lot?
Did someone know only one means to show the
love?
Did someone still keep something even when I
said meals I'll have not?
Did someone even when I returned at midnight
asked if something am to have?

This four-course meal doesn't match the high
standards you showed me,
And worse is to choose from this book called
menu which is no thinner,
The best place to have dinner is where you'd be,
And no menu matches the fun of asking, 'Mom,
what's for dinner?'

Most meals were repeat of the days past,
Predictable was taste and guessing the items was
no brainer;
Having eaten at countless fine dine in and joints
fast,
Can certainly say nothing matches what used to
be for dinner.

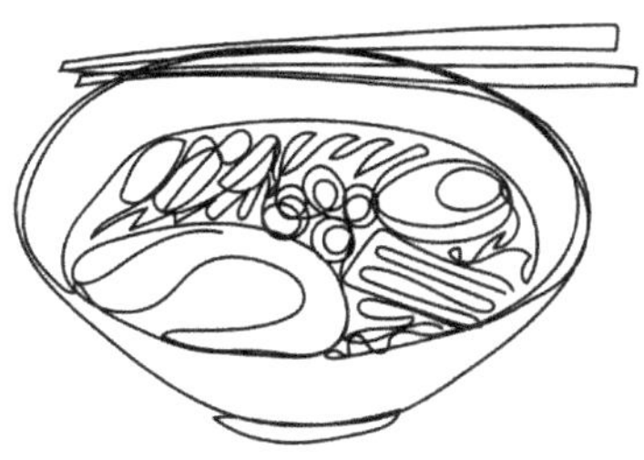

That Cricket Match

I have never held a bat on field but the game
fascinates me like none,
The stylish 11 trying to stop one man to score is
a treat to watch,
A game which is of team and yet could be of
one,
A game in which the exhilaration goes beyond
the notch.

My home becomes a stadium of its own on
every big day,
And this was no different when India met the
rival arch,
Gathered were at my place self-appointed
experts of game to say,
From pitch to field to cloud to squad, they had a
view on the match.

And thus started the game and it turned true to
its promise,
The green rivals made a mountain to be scaled,
At least one or two top batsmen need to stay till
end that was the premise,
While all showed promise but eventually failed.

Swung the match like a pendulum till the end,
Stood one star against the odds and that kept the
hope alive,
At one end was fall of wickets with little support
to lend,
Moved this hero like a champ and he did thrive.

The match went till the over last and resulted in
a win,
Thrilled were we beyond and the star became
God incarnate,
Some discussed his stroke, some resolved to dig
in,
Slowly spoke the oldest man in the room with
clarity straight.

"You know why we won? Because he stayed till
wicket nine,
His companions fell but he was hard to deceive,
They tried to trick but he read them and crossed
the line,
Because just like in life, only those survive who
know what to leave."

Tasks would challenge, and opportunities would
tempt you,
Obstacles would mock and people would test;
But in the end, it's noise outside versus calmness
inside you,
The outcome determines if you are a winner or
like the rest.

The 20 Rupees Note

"Is it the final price?" asked the boy with a tone
sounding as a request,
"It's the price, saying for the time third", the
frustrated shopkeeper exclaimed in a fit;
Could see a young boy with sub ordinary clothes
standing desperate and in quest,
His one hand on the book he wanted to buy and
second a tightened fist.

Slowly loosened his wrist could, see a crumpled
Rs. 100 note,
"I have got this much", now the tone softened
even more,
Shopkeeper was hesitant, "I told you kid, it is
short.
You need to bring Rs. 20 more."

I slid my hand in my pocket and pulled out one
he needed,
Someone wants to study and for a single note
shouldn't be sent away,
I placed my currency over the book he wanted,
The boy looked surprised but too overwhelmed
for anything to say.

I only smiled and his eyes brimmed with
happiness replete,
I understood, "Oh please don't mind, it's just
rupees twenty,"
The boy slowly murmured, "Sir, this small note
actually made my big note complete.
If only a small amount can flow to those who
need from those who have plenty"

The world should run on hard work and not on
charity,
But those with less sometimes need only a little
more
And I don't fancy any dreamworld equality,
But painful is to see over a hundred rupee bill, a
rupee 20 note score.

PART Ⅲ
The Breeze

The Gathering

This dates back to years ago but common to
each locality,
There lived a different city in each city which
came out at a specific time;
All the people would gather from the vicinity,
And the place would become like a fair prime.

Would be discussed what wasn't working in the
country,
And would soon get changed to which batsman
needs to be dropped;
Some would discuss how much traffic infra has
become crumbly,
While one would tell the story of theft in a house
locked.

The kids would have a different joy,
Giggles of some would get mixed with howls of
some;
The look stealthily that girl gave to the boy,
And yet it would get noticed by some.

And suddenly the place would become bright
and illuminating,
"Light is there" would sound like a war cry;
A country of different colors used to get united
by load shedding,
An event of pain used to become moment to
enjoy.

The Mandatory Birthday Celebration

There are a few mails that can scare you a lot,
When the sender is from the most loved team,
that is HR.
And the title of the mail is an event which is of
celebration for the most,
Yet for me it has been a rather passable hour.

Sometimes we clap for a person we barely know,
Many times we in crowd can hardly hear or
view,
Most times we know the rituals' flow,
All the times we know, what's the menu.

This time too I was not having a mountain of
expectations,
As always, the place was full up to the brim.
I was standing quietly waiting for
commencement of 'presentation',
Came a low voice from behind, "From this side
you can't swim".

I turned back to find a team member new,
Most recently joined and is still getting
introduced;
"What swim?" I asked, "I'm sorry I didn't get
you",
He looked around, leaned and softly said,
"Something, I have deduced!"

"What is the most important part of this
celebration?"
"Birthday person. Some speech…" I was saying
but was interrupted,
"No! The crunchy samosa, fluffy dhokla, spongy
cake", was his exclamation,
"And as perfect investors we should maximize
returns", he instructed.

Said I, "Well! No need for so much stress, you
would get it like everyone",
"Ah! That would be one piece each; What if you
want another?"
"Then you ask again", in this conversation I was
losing fun,
"But then you get seen as a hog in the office
party", said the man wiser.

"Plus, what if our mission is to conquer Mount
Samosa before anyone?"
"All samosas taste the same", I was finding it
funny,
"Aha! But here you have the first chance to say,
'much better than earlier one."
With mandatory celebration comes calls for
contribution mandatory,

"What's the plan?" I laughed for I never saw it
this way,
"We are at southeast, the target is in the direction
northwest;
We would get two chances to traverse the array,
Would move three steps when each speaker is
called", said the strategist best.

"Remember we are doing it for honor, glory and
greater good",
"Of course! What if the samosa is bad? We are
saving others", I added;
"Wonderful! You are a quick learner, I can trust
you and I would",
For the first time I was doing something so silly
but fully motivated.

The first speaker spoke about the importance of
such days,
We reached till cake by the time; The second
one gave lessons and tales;
By then, we made a strategic turn towards the
cutlery and trays,
Were at vantage before the third one, all by just
outpacing the snails.

And we did right check all the options with ace,
Took samosas twice without being noticed,
Praised the HR for the Leadership;
A sheepish smile remained all through on the
face,
Said I, "Louis, I think this is the beginning of a
beautiful friendship."

Interesting, Exciting, Encouraging

Ever got pulled in a meeting unplanned?
The agenda not told in advance yet need to
contribute,
And there are people from all levels and
command,
So you have to say something and attribute

The first plan should be to duck,
For why to make the obvious what can be
concealed:
But if you are running out of luck,
Here are the secrets of survival revealed

There should be three silver arrows in your
quiver,
These are Interesting, Exciting and Encouraging;
Advice is to use them to sound as winner,
Can place you comfortably without committing
a thing

The first arrow is to be used when the subject
you don't understand,
Can term any point or position interesting;
Would be in no pressure to negate or justify your
stand
And for many you would shine with a halo ring

The second one is to salute the grade,
Once a powerful takes a view, it's time to use;
Term the opportunity exciting and plan well
made,
Quote that it's a case difficult to refuse

The third one is for self-defence,
Often would be asked about status of things in
past;
Encouraging are the trends if seen from different
lens,
And this how difficulties you can outlast

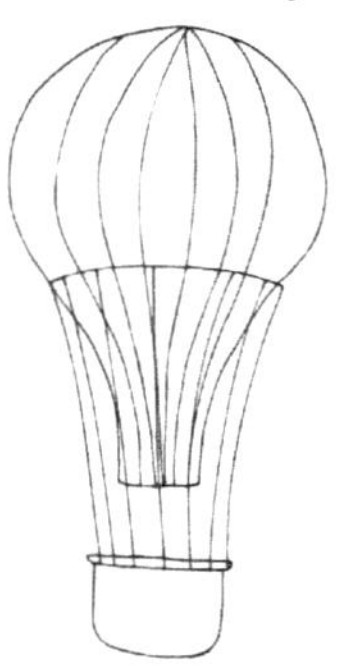

Piece or Peace

Those stories in childhood, those fascinations of
young life,
Those celebrations in the classrooms, those
victories in the competition;
One has to be a conqueror no matter the price
For winning is everything and is beyond
question

Life is a pyramid learnt this lesson ages ago,
Few get mentioned even in the school roll of
honour;
As you adult, the arena becomes battle for solo,
Winner takes all, competence just a good point
to ponder

Read books replete with tales of emperors,
Who waged wars for territory and the gold;
But what if I want to be a different conqueror,
What if I want to mend the definition old?

What if I don't want to get the crown by a cloak
dagger,
What if I don't want to be a king;
What if I want to be an example and a leader,
What if I want to chase a purpose and not a thing

What if I want to be a warrior who doesn't tire
down,
What if I just want to smile come what may;
What if I don't want to own the richest grave in
the town,
What if I just want to live the day

What if I want to make a different choice,
Want to win the morning dew and celebrate the
moonlight;
What if the rains and sun make me rejoice,
What if I want to win the internal fight

What if I want to live each second as a lifetime,
What if I don't want to wage war for gold's
piece;
Hope this wouldn't be seen as a grave crime,
If over everything, I choose happiness and
peace

The Forgotten Trophy

Yes, today was again not your day,
The list again got made leaving you;
May be you started fine but now lost the way
Or maybe what others say is actually true

Before you decide to put yourself in a category,
May I take you to a place you own
It is something you forgotten as the ordinary
It was yours but you left as you had grown

Every house has a place which stores the things old,
Ones which don't serve today but once were of importance;
The things which could neither be given nor were sold,
They represent your past, they are mirrors of your significance

Pick up that old trophy which you won at school ground
It no longer shines but it still glows
Those moments when hundreds clapped as your name got announced
You are this trophy even in your lows

Do you remember those three morons who
yelled the most,
They were and are still your friends, don't you
know;
And you were congratulated even by the one
who lost,
There were special ones who wished you after
the show
And you had brought this one home like the
World Cup,
Your mother cheered and so did the sibling;
But strange was the reaction of the man who
would often snub,
The seldom speaking father wouldn't stop for a
thing

You are the same soul even if time has changed,
Don't listen to false criticisms and sympathies
phoney;
You have gained lessons and not just aged,
You can lay hands on success says this trophy

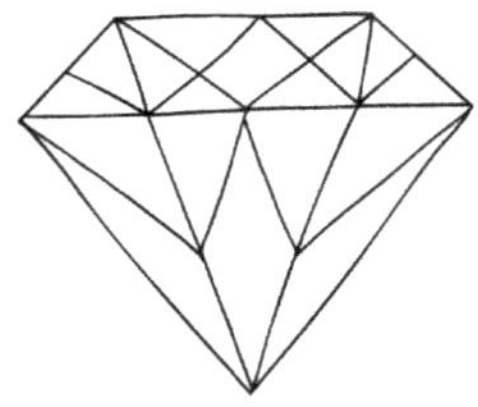

The Confession

I come in different colours, I have different
names,
Recognized every time, needed everywhere,
And yet I'm the one who's put often to blame,
There are deities of me and also been called
Devil's share.

They say I fueled evil and pain,
And then they say I am the reason for wonderful
endeavors,
Some say I'm a creation of God and some call
me human gain,
Even those who hate me want my favor.

I'm money.

They say I rule the world,
They say I drive the sin and fire the rage,
I divide the blood, make relations curled,
I am the war, I was the war in all times and age.

But honest confessions I do want to make,
I was to be in pocket, who took me to heart,
I was to be in mind, who to head did take
I'm worshipped with Gods, yet prefixed with
dirt?

Who says I'm needed in plenty?
Who says I can't just be in sufficiency?
I'm neither creator of an arrogant mind nor of
soul empty,
Why can't I just be considered one more element
of human agency?

In reality, some want me to compete with God,
While some want me to embarrass the devil,
To tell you honestly, I just want to flow to a
different abode,
And then I'm called unreliable.

The Postcard

Do you remember me? As I don't get seen often,
Once I was so ubiquitous, that not having seen
me was hard;
The pale yellow color was part of every house,
amazed how fortunes have fallen,
Once the trusted messenger of this country, I'm
the Postcard.

Used to cost less than an average candy,
How to write on me was taught in schools as
part essential,
Just an open piece of cardboard I used to travel
places many,
I was the messenger of hope, love and peace,
that was my credential.

On me, hearts were written, emotions were
woven all over,
My khakee carrier was treated like a family
member;
People used to write till the last inch and readers
to read over and over,
For some I brought the first love, for some the
last sombre.

And all over, it was open, cheap and
unconcealed,
I travelled the world and no one other than the
recipient would read,
I was not meant for today's world where trust is
distant and mistrust is all revealed,
Not meant for the world of password on
messages and intentions concealed.

I belonged to a world where the actions had
transparency,
And so there was so less to hide;
The moral code of each human was guarantor of
privacy,
Couldn't have existed in a world of present
divide.

Rasmalai

Take yourself to that summer afternoon when
from school you just returned,
"Mom, what's in lunch?" you yelled while
throwing clothes in all corners,
And Mom did not listen in one go, or chose to
be unperturbed,
And lunch would be one boring vegetable, to it
none of us would be foreigners.

Some days would be special, as it would be a
treat,
Though most days would be like the one before.
But special would be a few days which are
differently sweet,
The lunch could be boring but they have
something more.

"Rasmalai, when did it come?" remember you
chirping,
"Today, but you have to finish the meals first",
mom would order;
And we would finish the vegetable without time
wasting,
And then would start work on mission broader.

Would observe the spongy ellipse submerged in
yellow sea,
The spoon will break one small piece, put in
mouth and close the eyes,
And slowly it would melt in bliss and every
other thought would flee,
Just like this, one needs to feel life.

Yes that one message which you receive from
someone dear,
Look at each word, read it and hear with eyes
closed,
And feel the taste of it as if given by someone
near,
And cherish it like a moment uncomparable,
ready to say adios.

Ageing Together

That one wrinkle, under the eye that one dark
line,
That one Grey hair, that would separately shine;
That face of beauty of an angel and peace of
sage,
Oh God bless me to live long to see her age.

That wisdom of decades dripping from each
spoken word,
The stiff knots getting untied in manners
unheard;
And her silence meaning more than a string of
words on a page,
Oh God bless me to live long to see her age.

That set of glasses on nose just to read in style,
That frown of not finding it and then picking it
up with smile;
And would love to just get her snap this while,
Oh God bless me to live long to see her age.

That gravity of time and yet exuberance of child,
That laughter of joy and that rebuke mild;
All would subside in company whether grief,
anxiety, pain or rage,
Oh God bless me to live long to see her age.

The Movie Show

Ladies & Gentlemen, you are welcome to the
show,
Hope you'll enjoy the time you have here.
As the show starts in no time, there are things
you should know,
So that you make the best of your time there.

There would be a lot of light, sound and music
in the beginning,
For the start is always different from the rest.
However, the story would take time in building,
Please be patient and don't worry about what
lies next.

There's a concessionaire for you to avail meals
of liking,
They would taste better if you like the movie.
Try to focus on what's on screen and not on
mobile blinking,
Yes, not every scene would be of your liking,
some even would be gloomy.

To refresh yourself and take stock, there would
be an intermission,
You can loudly express about the show.
But once the show restarts, please focus again,
that's submission,
What you see next would be same as the past,
the chances are low.

Once the movie ends, please exit calmly,
Most of you won't be seeing each other again.
You all have come for the same show but all
would see a different story,
This movie is titled "Life", welcome again.

The Summer Rains

"The breeze is damp, somewhere it must have
rained,
Would have quenched the soil, drenched people
at large;
With me crossed seven decades, I can say with
mind trained,
There are seasons and there are the summer
rains.

Clearly remember holding hand of someone
special,
Holding one umbrella and we were partly dry,
largely wet.
Flew those days like the breeze gentle,
And so did the special one, but the days I can't
forget.

Then there were days where wishes had wings,
'Next rainy season will do the camping', I would
announce.
Would go on long drive may be in a car bigger
with fancy things,
These were also the memories I can't renounce.

There were days at home taking the view from
balcony,
Sipping a few hot drinks and admiring the colder
wind,
The time would pause like there isn't rush any,
Making every moment a bliss which doesn't
rescind.

But what do I miss the most,
Walking in the rain without umbrella with pals,
Jumping and dancing at will for nature was our
host,
And leaving behind expectations, sorrows and
all.

Have lost touch with those who were ready to
get drenched with me,
Some taken away by age, some by work and
some simply on different paths went;
But if age has given me any better vision to see,
Time is what with friends gets spent.

Then sarcasm didn't have any hidden concern,
That carelessness that not everything is worth
much pains,
Those freely exercised rights over each other,
which one had to earn,
And that roaming like rulers of the world in the
summer rains."

And then stopped speaking the old man who I
was standing next,

We were waiting for taxi at the hospital
premises;

I was there for some routine health test,

He was leaving after getting a terminal disease
diagnosis